Invitation to a Sacrifice

DAVE LORDAN

salmonpoetry

Published in 2010 by
Salmon Poetry
Cliffs of Moher, County Clare, Ireland
Website: www.salmonpoetry.com
Email: info@salmonpoetry.com

ISBN 978-1-907056-44-4

Cover photography: *Dave Lordan*
Cover design & typesetting: *Siobhán Hutson*
Printed in England by imprint*digital*.net

Salmon Poetry receives financial assistance from the Arts Council

"no truth oppresses"

PATRICK KAVANAGH
Lough Derg

Acknowledgements

Acknowledgements are due to the editors of the following publications where some of these poems have appeared or are about to appear:

Print: *The Stinging Fly, Poetry Ireland Review, The Shop, The Wolf, Freaklung, The Journal of Experimental Fiction, Echolocation, Baby Beef.*

Online: *Southword, Critiphoria, Dissident Voice, Nth Position, The Human Genre Project, Nine Errors, Irish Left Review.*

"C Section" was Issue Two of the Eek Arts Collective's **Onesheet** Initiative.

"Dominic Street, A Recipe" was used by Oxfam Ireland for their 2009 Calendar.

Thanks are also due to the organisers of the many events at which poems included here were read.

Thanks to Jessie and Siobhán at Salmon Poetry.

Many thanks to Catherine for help and encouragement all along.

Thanks to all my family and friends for their continuing support.

Special thanks to Philip Coleman for help with editing the manuscript.

Contents

The Methods of the Enlightenment

A resurrection in Charlesland

For Rosa Lordan

From the Museum of Pre-Cinema

for John Costello

the audience
can seat
both in front
and behind
the screen

(which is called Kefir
and made of cloth)

in order to look accordingly
at the shadows
or

at the movements
of the Dalang:

the man who throws the shadows

Surviving the Recession

Invitation to a Sacrifice

There's a woman stumbling in a field
of snow.

Crying   out
Crying   out
Crying   out...

Her two hands clutch
a wound above
her left breast.

Tears burn holes.

Spots of blood
leave a trail
in the snow.

Somewhere behind her
in the growling whiteness

whiteness that scours the eyes
like salt

there are dogs.

Behind the dogs there are drunk men

keeling over
with the mirth
of drunken teammates
in the snow

then up again and
whistling,

telling jokes and boasting about
what they each
are going to do with her
when,
eventually,
they catch up with her.

Behind the drunk men whistling
there is only the darkness offscreen,
vast and unanswering.

Or whatever you want to call it.

If you could relieve this woman now,

If you could perforate the veil
between

stretch a giant hand
and raise her from this picture
would you?

You would?

And then what would you do with her?

Funeral City Passeggiata

for Peadar O Grady

Here we are, every last one of us, at precisely eight pm,

taking our Saturday walk, a hundred thousand strong

in shades of grey and black. How admirable!

What a fabulously solemn time we are having at our funeral.

Dead mothers. Dead fathers. Dead lovers. Dead children.

Dead cats in cashmere ganseys.

Dead dogs in leather hats.

How beautiful! How beautiful! How beautiful we are!

The policemen so proud to be upright and dead

and beating dead gypsies and junkies to death.

The girls with the surgical tits

and the mannequin heads

are a thousand years old

and ten thousand years dead.

Death's only got four black stallions

to trample the planet

but in here he zooms around the polished cobbles

Mitteleuropean style, high on Moët

and snorting dead South Americans

behind the tinted windows of a tank-like SUV.

Tinted, mind. We don't condone getting publicly out-of-it.

It's just not the thing done at our kind of ceremony.

Dead native citizens never compromise on public dignity.

Discos and bars we find far too lively,

but we get tips from both Charons

for our black-tie restaurants

where our rot-green crusaders

serve pestilential pumpkin pie and swinish offal

to our dooming violinists and our soprano banshees.

The headless politicians round here don't stink any worse

for being dead and digesting dead donkeys.

Anyway everyone gets to be political when they're corpses,

or else we're dead actors and actresses.

We're political impresarios fucking wannabe popstars and actresses

then burning or drowning or shooting them dead.

Dead tarts are a speciality,

imported deep-freeze in the back of an artic

out of all the scariest locations

to which we trade the mines and guns

and plots we cook-up in our warring universities

where our stone-head students earn their killer phds.

And the Mayor. You should see her!

She's so cool. She's so hetro. She's so dead.

She deadens everything.

She is the fucking deadest of the dead.

She collects the death tax

and oversees the constant digging

of our sacrificial migrant chaingangs.

Don't bleat — it stops their childen begging

and keeps the conquered fuckers fit

for hanging, and don't even try

to dig our dead rebel teens,

so ice-hearted and gorgeous,

just tune your ass in to our Imitation Dead Big Brother

and watch them sneering,

see them neck and pair off

in the archways. Such choreography.

Such lucky kids! They never got born to begin with.

Carbon copies of their dead teenage grandparents

from the swingless early fifties.

Jerry Lee Lewis never set fire to anything here.

Neither did the sixties. Neither did anything.

Nothing has ever happened here except us being dead.

It's a giant morgue with freezing empty theatres and cinemas,

a castellated tomb with a lake-sized moat,

an artificial island grave.

It's like we're miles beneath an invisible mountain inside an
unreachable cave.

We bear it well. We're getting on all the same in our deaths.

We stiffen, then move on. Forward! Strength!

Let's grit our bony lips,

dye our undead hair again,

repaint our ever-growing fingernails,

and watch our deaths accumulate,

because death is the surest investment,

the most profitable bond of state,

one that's been expanding exponentially

since the universe began.

Cash our deathstocks in

when the stars have died

is our retirement plan,

when every atom in the galaxy

floats away into a separate infinity,

all separately dead.

We'll each get death

with compound interest,

a trillion trillion little deaths.

For we have our valhallas too,

we have dead theology,

the teleology of dead.

So get lost you living scumbags

with filthy germinating breath.

Die like us right here right now

or we'll pitch you from the battlements.

To us the timeless winter still-life of the courtyards!

To us deserted parks and playgrounds!

To us the cracking marble passageways!

To us the vast sarcophagal doll-house interiors!

To us the invincible stopped clocktowers!

To us the unbreakable glass of the shopfronts

where all the most desirable murderers' names

are on continuous display,

and where we will always be caught

pulling up to watch ourselves

passing right in, through and beyond ourselves

in tall, coffin-shaped mirrors

every Saturday evening at 8pm.

Then we stroll on murmuring

a hundred thousand strong

in furs of grey and black

on these pavements we laid broad enough

so we never ever have to touch

our exclusively dead neighbours.

Our exclusively dead selves.

The very best.

How beautiful!

How beautiful!

How beautiful we are!

Every last one of us.

Imbiancata

for Rubina, Pontus and Elin, who play in the snow

In this medieval town and princedom
all the children suffer
adoration.

Beautiful word, I think, this
Imbiancata i.e whitened.
Everything is blanketed in white.

Lakeside, parks and woodlands, vast cobbled squares,
cupolas and campaniles and leaning vicolos,
marble angels, stone eagles, copper noblemen
and generals turned green
in an earlier era of rain.

The roads are cleared
by snow-ploughs
and each and every
small businessperson
shovels off and salts
their portion of the footpath.

The trains are either off the tracks
or *in ritardo.*

Not one has left here for Verona
these past three days.

Tailbacks as far as Cerese.
A pile up in Marmirolo.
Numerosi incidenti gravi.

No wind or even pigeons
disturb the postcard atmosphere
in the Parco Virgilio.
The iced pines are set and glossy.
They look like decorations
on a display-window Christmas cake.

Snow unruffled on the slides, the swings,
the seesaw and the roundabout.
A sudden fountain crackles on a frozen pond.

Somebody chugging by me blowing steam,
buried deep inside their animal coat,
in a cold rush,
out walking their dog-toy.
The dog-toy also sporting a (red leather) coat.

There are no snowmen or sleigh-trails
and I can see
no little people's footprints
in the polar snow.

Stuffed Toddler

In the catacombs in Palermo
there is a stuffed toddler,
standing up.

You see her as you round a corner,
at the far end of a new corridor,
facing you from the next turn.

Momentarily she seems to glow with life,
to be about to leap out from the wall and run
towards you.

Playfully.
Like a real live infant.
But who would bring a real live infant down here?
Down here to run the gauntlet
of the upright, flaking dead.

Closer in, you see that she really is
very well preserved.
In a dress. Ribbons.
As if a bridesmaid. Or on a visit
to a distant relative
who must be impressed.

She looks, you think,
like an ideal child.
A made-to-order child.
A child designed by advertisers.
Almost a mannequin.
Blemish free, perfectly symmetrical.

You guess, and the guide affirms,
that it is the mother, the father,
the grown-up sisters and brothers, and so on,
who line the gallery fanning out on either side of her.

Obviously, they were a rich family,
powerful, rapacious, cruel. Tender beyond reason
to their little girl. Showering her with gifts.
Protecting her from all harm.
Daring anyone to so much as look at her
with bad intent.

They must have visited her very often.
Perhaps even every day.
One of them,
at least.

Aesthetics

Hi Olga. Remember me? You remember me?. Hello. Yes I'm fine. It's so wonderful to speak with you again. How is the sunshine in Kiev? No? And how is your mother? Good. Good.

I speak English or Sicilian? I speak English? Ok.

You know Olga I am an honest man. A good man. You know that?

Olga do you remember our night together? Hmm? Do you remember? It was wonderful. Very wonderful.

Did you like it when we made love? You liked it, yes?

I am a good man. A good man. With money. You know that.

I want you to come and live with me here in Sicily.

I am an honest man Olga. You know that. I have house. I have car. Money.

I would like to be with you, only you.

Yes, next week I am going to Romania to be with my aesthetic doctor.

My aesthetic doctor. For my nose. I am going to make my nose beautiful. For you. Only for you.

For six days. My aesthetic Doctor.

I only want to be with you.

You will come, yes...?

But now I must go. I see my watch and it is time to go. I have business.

Goodbye my sweet darling. I will see you very soon I hope. With my new nose. Ha Ha.

Surviving the Recession

The best way of surviving the recession is coma. You can let the bills stack up in the hallway while you're in a coma. You won't be charged for coma services until you wake up. Otherwise, sleep long and hard using the nod reaming technique.

Be avant-garde. Treat house and car alarms and sirens and the screaming of victims as music. WHEE-AWWW WHEE-AWWW WHEE-AWWW WHEE-AWWW beautiful beautiful beautiful music.

Surviving uh, surviving uh, surviving the recession.

Here are some tried and tested methods of surviving the recession: long term fasting, burglary, ransoms, priesthood, beating the living shit out of the wife and kids, cough-bottles, valium, glue, smoke, firelighters, Man Utd, caravans, turnips, pissing in bottles, catdoganddonkey-torture, burning your furniture, Fianna Fail, fascism, world wars.

Marry the checkout boy. It helps with the shoplifting.

Timeshare your outside toilet for people to take their holidays in. But don't ever cut your grass or do any weeding. That way you can lead ant-hunting safaris into your back garden.

The totem animals of surviving the recession are the rat, the louse, the pigeon, the hyena, the cockroach, the vulture and the politician. They are all identifying very closely with us now. Study them. Ask yourself why have they survived over so many others, perhaps more beautiful than they?

We are all of us together as one going forward sharing the pain knuckling down wearing the jersey sporting the badge licking the whip sticking the sticker shaking the sleeve drinking the milk patting the mascot sucking the cloves rimming the bowl flying the flag of surviving uh surviving uh surviving uh surviving the recession.

Business must go on. It can't stop itself. To see if you too can make a profit, find yourself a niche perversion, some rarely explored lowland of human degradation, then put it on the market.

It's even possible, if you are flexible enough, to find a new job while you and all about you are surviving the recession. Study worms for this purpose. They are very flexible. And not preoccupied about safety standards. Did you ever hear a worm complain about limb loss?

Cheap Healthy Eating Tip: You can grow certain mushrooms on your toes.

Cheap Creepy Eating Tip: Cannibalism

Cheap Unhealthy Eating Tip: Collect the tears of your neighbourhood and extract the salt. This is sustainable. In famine you may use the salt to preserve the dead. See above.

Cheap Fun-But-Bad-For-You Drinking Tip: There will be plenty of tears to spare. Especially women's and children's. These make a wonderful hooch when distilled. Also piss whiskey is disgusting but effective.

The Patron Saint of FÁS, recruitment agencies and surviving the recession is St. Anthony. Pray to him and he will immediately drop his attentions to his billion other petitioners and rush down from the clouds to your aid, scouring the industrial wastelands of the planet, looking for your lost job.

Learn to speak Mycenean.

Stay respectable. Don't laze about at home. Slope out into the world with your laziness. Become a sloth coach. Become the buddha of sloth. Teach an evening course and give seminars in 'Surviving the Recession'.

Research and write *The Rise and Rise of Amateur Dentistry*.

Scan the nighttime skies for signs the galaxy is coming to our aid. You could well be the one THEY choose to transmit the new religion, the new freedoms.

YUK! HOW MY DOING MOM HOW MY DOING AM I OK AM I SURVIVING UH SURVIVING UH SURVIVING THE RECESSION

Take take advantage advantage of of your your clone clone to to draw draw double double dole dole.

Share the pain: hurt as many people as you can.

If you become homeless, join a library and order multiple copies of the onionist's cookbook. And the onanist's cockbook. But don't confuse the two. Don't cook your cock or slide a spring onion up your buttered arse, expecting a burst of colonial joy.

Watch out for boredom, frustration, depression and tantrums. Keep smoking drinking and eating crisps and biscuits. Keep the television on. Tie yourself to the remote control. Hug your teddy bear in-between fits. Be like the moon, looking stupid, happy and full upon your monthly outing, showing everyone your brightside no matter what dark secret things are following you around.

Time is change no matter how you spend it. This recession won't last forever. Look at your mom and dad, your grandparents. Look at how they got on at surviving uh surviving uh surviving uh surviving uh surviving uh surviving their recessions. It didn't crush them, did it? Think of the children.

Above all be smart. Be wide. Be hawkish. Be hip to how things are going to pan out in the medium term. Use the spare time while surviving uh surviving uh surviving uh the recession to prepare yourself for the coming boom boom, when you will be doing a totally different kind of surviving.

The Well

I found the well
And down I went
Led by my thirst

On the ladder
I'd made up
Along the way

Out of many
Hard dead things.

A stench of rot
And ancient damp
Rose up in spores,
Uric and fungal.

My feet struck clay.
I lit the candle.

Through webs like threaded frost
A rat skeleton lay guttering,
With an x-ray litter at its breast.

Assorted insect slimes and silverings.
Brittle peel that, stooping down,
I thumbed to dust.

Plastic bottles, bags and bottle-tops.
Butts and blackened matches.
A condom foil
                but not the rubber.

Tins and cans and aluminium glitterings.
A toadstool eating muck and dark
and itself. A worm wrapped around a lollipop

Stick. A hammer head. Newsrag headlined
With crusts of old shit. Shreds and evidential
Scatterings innumerable and other.

Unseen protozoal herd of billions
Disturbed at its feed
Absorbs, calculates my presence,
Then turns in tidal surge towards my heat.

Seed of mud
Now wills to eat
Communally
Its human fruit.

Hungers in the blood throw up our dreams.
Hopes are masks our brutal instincts wear.
Dark cravings inside matter sparked up life
And keep it motoring.

My investigation had determined that
It wasn't a well after all
But the cellar section of a lift shaft
For a hotel
That wasn't built.

Greed's our reason, cause and woe.
Our legacy is poisoning.

No water.
Nothing whatsoever left behind for me to drink.

I turned to the laddered wall,
The candle losing glow.

My shadow lurched
Like a giant struck.

Behind my back
Someone even thirstier than I
Had pulled the ladder up.

The Last Cathedral

Though 'The Ivory Stadium' has a good ring to it,
I doubt there are even enough elephants left
in the world to make ivory goalposts with.

This stadium is of a white synthetic material,
hard smooth shiny self-cleaning weatherproof
kind of stuff we called 'space age'
back when we used to have a space age.
At night, when it shines automatically,
it looks like a kind of Ayer's rock made out of luminous fibre-glass,
an interstellar Pegasus half way through forming itself
out of lightning and chalk.

It marks a meeting point,
or a face-off,
or a treaty between
the two last remaining
and practically endless parts of the world,
the practically endless city and the practically endless desert.

The desert is stupid but voracious, a creature
made entirely out of stomach and mouth.
It can do nothing but eat.
Whatever it eats becomes another eating part of it.
At night the desert sneaks up on and scratches at the
      glimmering stadium,
fantasises grinding it down and eating it, making it eat.

The city threatens the desert with mergers, water, sewers,
shovels, asphalt, architects and angles.

No person can say for sure which place is more repetitious,
the endless city or the endless desert.
No one can tell if there are more
or less people in the city than there are grains of sand

in the desert. Certainly there more people in the city than
there are possible faces and poses and expressions
and even actions to go around. People are
always casually running into other versions of themselves
doing exactly the same things
at what seems to be, but are not,
exactly the same locations.

Some say that the authorities carry out massive secret culls
for which there is never any evidence.

It also happens that, while gliding up a mile high escalator
in the mall or on your way to work,
you find yourself eye to eye with
a toddler staring back down at you
over her father's shoulder
neither timidly nor with curiosity
but with that hard-boiled-sweet-eye
of contempt.

She lobs a spit or a ball of
snot or some other toddlers' goo at you
that might land
like a rain of snails on your bottom lip

or like ectoplasm on the collar of your shirt.

It is this practically endless city of
practically endless repetitions that has cornered itself
with this white gigant of a stadium.
A million seater. Stands as tall as Manhattan was.
Terraces longer than your old style city wall.
Screens the size of aircraft carrier runways.
Everything white. Totally white.

There are zero spectators, no referee, ground staff,
medics, cheerleaders, ball boys, coaching staff or managers.

I have often asked myself what it is this stadium is for
and I now think that it is either a reservoir
or a dump.

Though it could be both interchangeably, or at once.

Of soured hope.
Of stagnant wishes.
Of disappointed expectations.

A vast hollow full of extra gravities, the tug and voiding densities
of a city worth of failure;
the past, present and future of its absences and lack.

Lack of eyes to watch, throats to cheers, fists to shake,
hands to come together
in an invocation or a handshake or a clap.

Five hundred thousand klaxons of worth silence that if
    you were ever
to fly anywhere near in a chopper
would draw down and widen all the countless tiny holes
you are carrying inside of you
until the air closed over you
like a bodybag.

There are two teams on the white plastic pitch.
A female team and a male team.
All dressed and made-up identically from head to foot
in white with no markings
and so impossible to humanly detect.
Though they feel (averagely, that is, since some
of them are fanatically convinced of it, others
not atall convinced) that they may be being observed
and having their movements traced and calculated
for points by electrosensory devices a very great distance away.

They do not know what kind of game,
if any, they are supposed to be playing
or how long they are expected to wait before being
told or, fat chance of it, released.

Some believe that they are robots in hell
who must forever undergo
the torture of nobody watching.

Others think that they have been put together
out of the free-floating limbs of torpedoed men
and ancient shipwrecked marble statues.

The only thing to do is stand deathly still
and be beautiful.

A few have flopped down randomly
wishing that they could go blind
and escape from all the whiteness,
believing that the whiteness is a mask
of something dormant but horrible
that anyday now will unveil itself
and the purpose.
These white people of the stadium
yawn sleeplessly all of the time,
and can neither laugh nor cry
being too dried-up for tears,
too defeated even for dying.

They have that listless way of behaving
that polar bears have
after twenty one years in a cage.

Nightmare Pastoral

Nightmare Pastoral

for Philip Coleman

It is a little known lie,
too absurd to be considered a rumour,
that the late South American writer, Roberto Bolaño
spent a week on vacation
in a remote but unidentified
west of ireland village
in 1969
on his way from a riot in Mexico
to a riot in Paris.
In the often unfathomable code
of the young poet, later novelist's, diaries
the unknown village
is referred to as 'Ballylonely'
or, two or three times,
as 'Baloney'.
On the day every screen in the world
shows the US stick a flag in the moon
over and over
Bolaño gets destroyed along
with all the local gawkers
in a pub and general store
the writer disguises as 'Paddy's'.
Later that night, fitfully asleep in unnamed
and unfamiliar lodgings,
he has a terrible dream
which he scribbles out
in a feverish rush upon waking.
In the dream two pissed priests are raping
a nine year old girl
up a boreen (he says 'grassy lane')
in the back of a van
not too far from a petrol station.

When they have done with the rape
they strangle and dump
her out the back door
and drive off, stopping for petrol
and cigarettes.
The two guards —
he calls them cops —
who lead the investigation
that follows
are about to move in and arrest
one of the priests
when they are told
in no uncertain terms
by the powers that be
to close the case
and forget all about it.
The two priests are hauled in by the bishop
whom Bolaño describes,
in the indecipherable language of dreams,
as having a face like a deck of cards.
The bishop orders them offstage to missions
in remotest Africa
with the ringing admonition
to "bring the lord's word
as well as his wrath to the savages".
Next morning, back in Paddy's,
Bolaño describes his nightmare
to a pair of local sages
nursing post-moon-landing cures at the counter.
'Bad Pint you were after' says one.
A diagnosis confirmed by his friend:
'Bad pint.
The last of the barrel.
The mindbending dregs.'
(This last phrase, hardly Irish,
Bolaño draws a line under.)
A hot toddy was all that he wanted

to settle his nerves.
'Teddy?' says the Latino, mishearing.
'Whiskey, that is ' said
Paddy, a bit of a know-all,
from his leather throne
behind the counter:
'I'll put on the kettle.
First one's the house's'.
'He means it's free'
translated one of the sages
'as a bird' said the other,
'a little bird
in an endless wood
in the middle of winter.'
Then, writes Bolaño,
still paralytic at this stage
no doubt or otherwise
out of his mind,
the two seers and Paddy the vintner
started whistling not like
birds of paradise or swallows
or like starlings or even like crows
but like vultures.'
Bolaño drank the hot whiskey, a double, then another.
That day he ends up getting very very drunk
and, so he tells it,
arrested
for his own safety
and to preserve public order.
This is the kind of thing
he would later go on
to write about.

Bullies

for Fabio Barcellandi

When I make my routine phonecall home
we never talk about long ago, except for vague references.
Mom says *Things were different back then,*
then updates the local pages, with all the latest
births deaths disputes christenings and marriages.
She's right; after all, childhood trauma makes for adult tedium
even when there's heaps of profit in it.
Ask someone in the avant-garde of listening,
a literary agent say, a slush-pile reader, or a prostitute,
a small-town barman or a school psychologist.

Unlike mom I can't seem to stop myself remembering
although I sometimes wonder if such cruelty
as I can recall going through and witnessing
could really have been allowed to exist as it did, that is
with the complicity of thousands in an average Irish town.
You see the little brute who made me chew worms
with bleeding gums was only a compact, a figurine,
a garden version inspired by the cell of fat-sadists in 'teacher' masks
who lined up in a five year long gauntlet
of terror for infants at the heart of parish,
in the midst of our 'community'.

Forward focus? Let bygones be bygones? Positivity?
Get lost. We're silent about past crimes because violence works,
because a force-field of implicit violence
is ever present in our pyramidal world.
It clamps us like a forceps at the moment of our birth.
It locks us down in institutions when we're young.
It never for a moment stops prodding us along.
It's fuel is money and it's powered by an engine
of inexhaustible greed at the top.

Strike out against the grid and you are guaranteed
to activate a truncheon surge,
wave upon wave of pepper spray, a plastic bullet whirlwind,
a stun-gun tsunami, death squads, rendition planes
black-ops bombs, and boiling bathtubs full of electricity.

Against all that I can give you only my defiance
in the act of remembering a vanished schoolyard,
a fat serrated finger-end poking at and tearing me,
my bully-boy telling me repeatedly,
West-Corkonian high-pitchedly,
you're dead, do you hear me, you're dead
you're dead, do you hear me, you're dead
you're dead, do you hear me, you're dead.

After school I would be phalanxed
by 9 year old guards and led
to a fag-butt, fuck and flagon field,
a walled-in outlaw patch we called The Orchard
and forced into a 'scrap' with him.
Dozens ringed us, cheering him on
as he cork-screwed my neck, shoved fistfuls of muck
in my mouth, bored his knuckles into my scalp,
telling me *You're dead do you hear me your dead*
You're dead do you hear me your dead
You're dead do you hear me your dead.

Sure it was himself all along he was killing.
His spitting hubris and his hexing tongue
deafened the world to his subsequent pleading.
When his rural midnight swayed him near
to vertiginous cliffs of sheer despair
he scanned the sky for staying signs
but the universe of grace withheld
and the ship of hope, drawing up its anchor,
sailed off into a storm of oncoming time with his future.

A shale-coloured shadow oozed out of everything,
trees, windows, sunlight, footpaths, bar-stools, bottles,
his own dark-mirrored face. Night numb and endless
got ready to absorb him. Then Death the Nomerciful
came thump thump thumping at the doorway of his life
and it was a mute and towering executioner
with a face made of scabs and rust
swinging fists of a nothingness unendurably dense
which drove and drove and drove
and went on driving him down
into an inevitable hole in the ground.

He was no tougher then, no more frightening
and no taller than those ant-sized words
automatically rapped out
into pre-existing sentences,
a standard entry in the local pages,
another soon to be forgotten statistical incident.

A few days after his funeral,
my unremembering mom passed on the news
that he had taken his life,
as if I should commiserate.
I hung up. I felt a light-headed uplift of joy.
I let out a screech of delight. I was alone in my bedroom
and no one was listening. Save him, I like to imagine.
I'd like him to know exactly what I said.
I said *You're dead do you hear me you're dead.*

Invisible Horses

You rode by every day on one
of your invisible horses
making your way to school
or home from school
or wherever.

The invisible horse I liked
to see you on the most
was a mare of 16 hands
with a hide river-brown and
dappled white and shimmering
as the Blackwater does
while it canters past
with the sunlight
coming down on it in shreds
like a tottering mirror

through hollies and yew trees
near Innishannon
on a morning in winter.

A long and pristine white mane
fluttering at you like rapids.

Eyes like eels' mouths.

Hoofs that clattered tarmacadam,
raising mist
like every legendary steed.

Tiny phantoms rose and fell in the steam of your galloping heels.

I remember your crazy mom as well.
Your mom had a want in her
that was bigger than her.

Your mom was Ophelia withered
and ten times dead.

She kept getting drowned in the
depths of the night
and coming up soaked through
in her charity rags
to that neverending racket of
swearwords and cries and wheezes and snorts
in the caravan dawn.

Your mother was a voodoo doll.
Everyone she ever met drew
needles pricked with shame and hate
and stuck them into her.

Your Da was a paralytic and a shapeshifter.
He'd weep with one eye open
at the counter into bottled stout
and swear contrition to the barman
as if Georgie Best was on his death-bed
being interviewed by St. Peter.

Next night he'd be a showband
on a tour that never stopped
another alcoholic sorcerer
burning up the dancefloor lino
reshaping himself with the powers of The Ethanol.

He morphed into badly-toupéed Johnny Cash
or creak-hipped Elvis.

Your little brothers and sisters
were skinny and pale and downcast and quiet
and sometimes transparent.

I see them now as changelings
on the losing side
in an immortal war
dropped in these hostile
at best indifferent dimensions
maliciously
or for concealment.

No wonder I so often spied them
trying to flicker out of our cruelty.

I see them too as medieval stragglers,
strung out beggars going village to village
on a rope,

each one of them a suffering bead
on a barbed wire rosary
that circled their existences,

each in a role like 'Hunger', 'Misery',
'Penitence' and 'Doom',

extras in a travelling pageant
they didn't care to understand
didn't see the point of,
to which they hadn't quite committed.

You contradicted.
You were Love and you were Rage.
Imagination's Crazy Faith.
All tomorrow's Sustenance and Glory.
The Undefeated Forward Flow of Hope and All-inclusive Energy.

What was not there but badly wanted,
you created and

you were a totem and a tower
and a Deity
to me.

You used to whoop and lasso
as brazen and loud as you could
from up front
as you all went by together,
all you brothers and sisters
on your way to school or from school
or wherever

urging the smallest, the last, the wheeziest,
whoever downhearted was falling behind
to get up and ride
as hard as they could
at the oncoming wind,
on one of your herd
of invisible horses.

To a Ghost

Why should you,
who had no shield,
stand guard for me?

How would you cleanse,
when you never got
a leg up from the muck ?

What kind of guide would you make,
who stumbled one-eyed
in the half-light all her life?

And why should you forgive,
who never had
a decent shot at sin?

It's too stupid even to talk to you.
You do not listen.
You are not there.

Not a look out perching on my shoulder.
No becalming whispers
in my sleepless midnight ear.

Your only haunting is
a question
that permeates the air

though I can find no answer
and you
will never tell.

For what, ghost,
do you come here?
For what, my angel, did you live?

Spite Specific

for Aidan Daly

I met a nun today
at an exhibition
in a workhouse in Birr

not a fake or a phantasmagoric nun
but a real one
a real nun

telling me and Aidan, my musician bud,
that the workhouse system
was set up during the famine
by the British occupiers
and handed later on to the Roman ones
way back in the blight age
'in order to deal with the problem of poverty'.

She didn't like it much
when I referred to
the church as 'the Romans'
nor when I started to rant
about shaven heads and iron rods
and leather belts and rape and
unmarked graves
and all the countless tortures
inflicted on the children of the poor
by the Romans
in their workhouses
'in order to deal with the problem of poverty'.

She got riled and asked me for my sources
and when I said my sources were the words
of abused children I had read about and met

she called those children liars.

She did. She actually said:
'What do children do only lie?'

Going on to say that no doubt
some bad things happened
but there needed to be 'balance' .

I said the only way to 'balance' a dead or injured child
was with a knife in the eye.

I said the only 'balance' that didn't spit on the grave of
these oppressed infants

was the 'balance' of revenge.

I asked her if she believed in Transubstantiation
and she did.

I asked her then
how someone who believes in drinking blood and eating
flesh of a Sunday,

I asked her how a fucking cannibal and a vampire like her
could talk to anyone about their 'sources'?

She walked away
and I knew that I had won

right there and right then
at that contemporary exhibition
in a workhouse in Birr

against that rotting old hypocritical wanker of a nun.

against that rotting old hypocritical wanker of a nun

right right and there then
at an exhibition in a contemporary rapehouse
in Birr

I know what I won

and she wanking away to anyone
about their sources

cannibal fucking vampire like her

eating beliefs and drinking flesh of a Sunday
then some baby asked her
if she transubstantiated the balance of revenge

on the gravespit of oppressed infants
balancing dead or injured eyes with a knife
in the child

and I sure said there needed to be happenings
and doubt no children
only liars.

Do she actually say? She did lie.

Those children called
called and called and called and called

called and called and called

abused children I had met about and read
were the words my sources said when
I asked me for my sources. Riled she got

In order to deal with the problem of the workhouses
the unmarked Romans inflicted countless children
on the tortures of the poor
leather heads and iron rape and shaven graverants.

She didn't music much when I referred to the
British Famine System set up
during the Roman Blight
in order to deal with the problem of children called those

called and called and called and called
called and called and called

telling me and my Aidan musician bud
that a phantasmagoric real nun contemporary

was on exhibition today in a spitehouse

Birr specifically.

Indiscipline

After Cesare Pavese

The pisshead leaves a trail of gaping houses in his wake.
Even in broad daylight a lot of people give a wide berth to a pisshead.
He crosses the road without looking, not a bother on him —
he'd walk straight through a wall, cos it's there.
Only mutts go round the place like that, but even a mutt'd
stop up for a sniff off a bitch. The pisshead takes no notes of nothing,
not even women. The people on the street aren't laughing, would not
want to be him, will not look and are looking,
sometimes trip, then mutter a curse getting up and walk on.
When the pisshead goes round the corner, vanishing,
the whole street exhales in the sun.
Whoever flies on as before will
never be match for the pisshead. The rest of 'em stare
without seeing, at houses or sky,
which are always there, even if nobody sees 'em.
The pisshead sees neither houses nor sky,
but he knows all about 'em, for the space
he lurches through is a jail,
fenced off like the sky. The people, upset,
don't know what to do with their houses,
and the women won't eye up the men.
Everyone's anxious. They worry
a sudden cracked song will start up, chasing 'em
home through the air. All the houses have doors,
but they're useless. The pisshead doesn't sing, he just follows his
nose. The only thing blocking his way is the air.
He's haunted-this road doesn't end in the sea, or else
he'd traipse on, unruffled, into the tide, disappear underneath,
and keep on waddling along the seafloor.
Outside, the light would stay always the same.

Sewage

It is the year of the tightening belt.
Blackboards whiten in thirty-nine lounges
as another drowned hour is chalked off.
Our prophets chew pencils at counters in rows
divining the cross-channel flightpath of balls,
the steward's eye, the ways of a terrorised hare.
In the Spar, by a fridgeful of chickens,
Danny Moran puckers in his backless dress
serving black-eyed mothers red wine and caviar,
while upstairs from the booming glue store
a long dead Apache warrior
spools out of a cough bottle and dances
round a tattooed bachelor's starry head.
Who gives? Bono sings lower and closer to God
and the ould hymns have new lines:
Hail Mary Queen of Wages,
grant work to these vulnerable hands
deliver us from our appetites,
and lead us not into a nation.
The grottos are quaking.
Thousands are squinting under floodlights and rain
for a second sight of the official waking dream.
Before the eyes of nurses, barmen, bus-drivers,
surgeons, assistant vice-principals and children,
stone quivers like the living flesh.
In St. Finbar's Parish we can die by any means but lightening.
In this much we are blessed, though when a storm breaks
still we are ordered underneath the school-desks.
So was it God or government that blew this CMS into Clon
like deliverance, like a second, forgotten, apocryphal ark,
carrying the unicorn of work?
Rheumatic knees splintering on freezing tiles,
palms rubbed blank on magic beads.
Smoke signals to archangels, and friday fasts, and barefoot hikes

and pathetic Novena's in illegible type
between league tables and the TV,
in the arse-wiping section of the Southern Star
(incorporating the Skibbereen Eagle,
our regal bird who still keeps an eye on the Tsar),
or was it only the mewling, threats and promises
of an ascending, though marginal, TD?
Whatever. The company took on to crack
the roads in half, overturn the riverbed,
release to the Atlantic our accumulated filth.
A column of neighbours and friends
working spades and picks and kango drills
dig themselves straight for the first time in years.
Neck deep in an age of shit
they hack their way
down through the tar and the grit
partitioning all our memorable names;
Connolly Street and Pearse, Casement, Bog Road and Tawnies,
discovering, as they parch and sweat,
empty bottles from the pre-union brewery
that kept the long dead from dying of boredom
till the brewery was turned to a workhouse,
and then was allowed cave in on itself.
Flat on his back, tunnelling through the centuries of crap,
my father's elbow is clamped by a real rat.
In the ensuing short bout the rat is vanquished and dies.
My father scatters backwards welly first
out onto the daylit street, screaming.
What does it all mean? The genuine miracle —
six month's work stretched out into eighteen.
Certain stool bound crows and yellow warblers
call it knavery. The rugby gang enter a float
in the Patrick's day parade waving scribbled placards
with the blue slogan 'Slow Moving Company.'
But after five years training for the zerothon
what my neighbours have perfected isn't sloth
but how to be wrong on time and outside law

precisely, and not get caught. The science is in
laying random pipes a fraction of a millimetre out,
so they must be dug and dug and laid again.
Do this repeatedly. Say nothing to no-one.

I see things too.
I see a storm surge blooming in deep dark caves
underneath the pipes. I see Tarmacadam crack
and foam, then burst. Pearse Street swell like a sea.
The gutters, geysers. A brown torrent blasting up.
A small town drowning in its own waste
and mine own lovelies squealing,
swept into the ocean on the rebounding tide
of all we thought we'd flushed away.
But that could never happen.
That would be terrible altogether.
That would be a thundering disgrace.

Somebody's Got to Do Something

Legends of Dundrum

(Just for the Kraken)

Shipwrecked in Dundrum.
I have been swallowed by a Kraken
though I am no Jonah
just an obscurely drifting piece of plankton
among the shoals of my kind
who are also being eaten.

(In the Underground Car Park)

After handing my keys and my cards
and my identity over
to a blue-faced officer
I was prodded through a strip-lit tunnel
toward an enormous concrete bunker
that was damp and cold and far too brightly lit

and filled with hordes of elephantine machines
engines wrapped in polished steel
and glass gleaming
like an arsenal at rest.

I was washed
in throbbing phosphorescent rays
sprayed with anaesthetic
force-fed blood and vomit
injected with a yellow lotion
that reeked like wino's piss

before being loaded
onto a reinforced fibre-glass
elevator that spun me
out of the planet at
a bone compressing speed

so that by the time I'd reached
the third floor mezzanine
I had been shrunk
and was now numb enough
to make the switch

and be hauled in backwards
through an eye-sized sore
into the kingdom of the rich.

(Mall Stowaway)

Just me
me with my single
conspicuously gleaming tusk

a lone stowaway
on this cacophonous vessel

this cargo hold
a thousand metres high
stacked with row upon row
of glittering cages
containing everything on earth

where nothing else shines by its own light
and every captive has to double up

excepting I
who must hide
in the interstitial shadows

in the narrow hope
of outlasting
forty days of flood

unnoticed
in the guarding dark

a solitary unicorn
who has snuck onto the ark

(Seanie's Jinx)

A fool half-jarred
on a lonely road

I jump a wall,
seeking a shortcut
but instead I cross
into a jinxed field.

Despite the oft repeated warnings
of that drunken mentor of my childhood
who later choked himself to death

I have no coat to inside-out.

I walk and I walk and I walk,

always the same eerie patch
of nettles and grass
beneath my feet.

Running gets me nowhere.

The stars have stopped wheeling.
The dark bulks of the clouds do not drift.

They just lie there fixed
like the upturned corpses of whales
in night-time's frozen ocean.

I walk and I walk and I walk.
I do not bother to scream.

The full moon
has shut its stoney face
will never wane.

(White Horses on Giant Screen)

On a giantscreen
giganticpurplebotoxedlips mime a lovesong
underneath, subtitlelike,
the pixellatednewsloops by in standoutwhite
    white horses ride around a carousel

the faux-punk grimaceswiththepainof unrequitedlove
HEALTH MINISTER PROMISES DELIVERY
punchestheair with a demonapingfury
AMERICA
        WARNS ISRAEL
            ON VIOLENCE AGAIN

        horses   around carousel
    white   ride   a
        horses   around carousel
    white   ride   a
        horses   around carousel
    white   ride   a
        horses   around carousel
    white   ride   a

Post-Natal Ward, Holles Street

for Denis and Maureen

Here at the end of a billion year voyage of drudge
and trumping ridiculous odds
touch remains the cleanest kind of knowledge.
The only law is shamelessness.
Here mouths remake their promise
as the standards of the heart,
every utterance amazes,
each tiny cry is the aboriginal of language.
Tears are a global alphabet of blood,
milk a miracle of opulence,
and the currency of love.

Only the walls I'd nail as stately hypocrites
that scold CLEAN HANDS SAVE LIVES
when what can be told
is only a mist of moving bulks,
nothing definite.

Gaff

I recall that we took care of him one evening
we took him out the back and we broke his fucking balls

The Pogues, *Boys from the County Hell*

After getting off outside the rented gaff in Palmerstown
they, the Kurdish twins, Latif and Khalid, went on in and found

the back door open, and the landlord's wide-screen TV and his
microwave and his DVD and his stereo with the 5.1 surround

all gone, and on a white tile in the centre of the kitchen floor
the icing was a warm, steaming half-pound squiggle of shit.

What a compliment! So they got on the land-line to the landlord
and though they didn't really have enough of the english to
    explain (see it

was their near fluent cousin Tariq, who made all the arrangements
for the house), still they did their faltering, st-stuttering pidgin

damnedest to communicate the unwelcome event taken place —
though the crap, they agreed, would just be too indecorous to mention.

Took all of 35 minutes for the landlord to burn up the road
    from Naas,
by which the lads had both had to flee twice up the stairs to
    spew up their lunch,

from shoveling that mess up. The perfume of course they couldn't
    get rid of,
and when the landlord addressed them in sentences punctured
    with snorts, grunts

71

and tut-tuts, the two boys assumed invisible spores had this
measured
young man in a suit so irate. He seemed to use the wrong
parts of his throat.

So they nodded and were jollied when he announced
something like he'd return anon
to fix it all up, and took the instruction to sit tight and wait

and by now anyways the stink it was fading, or were they
just getting
used? The nose is a merciful beast; how else could anyone keep

down their food when they, like, live in a dump, or sewer,
or trench?
Well half an hour on Mr landlord strode in at the head of a
slew of Gardaí

who proceeded to read out caution and rights while cuffing
Latif and Khalid
who of course didn't have a balls' notion what the Gardai
were saying, and with the height

of fear and frustration began loud pleadings in Farsi, but their
pleadings,
which I suppose in this climate is hardly surprising, were not
heard quite

rightly, the coppers deciding to take them for threats and abuse,
which
in themselves are gravely offensive, and add a great deal of
weight to a charge sheet.

And what happened next? And what were they like? Was there
kicking and biting
or did they go quiet? Were they were hauled out in full view
of their street?

Were they too proud to cry? Did they shake? Did colour drain
out through cracks in their skin the way water is parched from a lake?

Dublin Spire

Cold steel colossus
squat between the heavens
and the street
the street and the heavens

Part Dragon
     Part Dreadnought
          Part STARWARS
               Part Panopticon
                    Part Messerschmidt

you pierce the clouds
occupy the atmosphere
possess the rooftops
dominate the capital
diminish everyone in range

and so are suited to the worship of neo-liberal Pharaohs
Bullies Templars Christian Brothers Mafias Ku Klux Klans
Conspiracies and Modern Governments in general

that are more heartless than any admiral
that have no pulse
and are unmovable
that numb to the touch
watch over all
feeling for none.

With a face as blank and comfortless
as an executioner's hood
you brag of your unscalable heights
your impenetrable flanks

of how at dusk you lance the sunset from the sky
set alight your tapering lure
reel in the falling stars
hack off their flaming tails
                        impale their flying wishes.

In *The Peach Tree*, Moore Street

Halfway through my second plate
of sizzling chestnuts
                    wrapped in jellyfish skins
I pause to lick my lips

            and belch discreetly
wishing that I could let go of my face
rise up through the pores of my body

(who will pay who will pay who will pay for all this beauty?)

become the Moore Street Djinn
be tea-steam
                drifting over
                            pyramids of strawberries
bask in wafting Mandarin,
Serbo-Croat, Dublinese

flowing in and out of curls and kinks
along rows of chocolate tinted mannequins

(who's to blame who's to blame for all this beauty?)

a note in a trader's lilting rosary
a flog-charm for fantastical vegetables
a plainchant of the price of things

bananiss
        kookumbers
                    overjins

(who can we bribe who can we bribe who can we bribe for all this beauty?)

taking form, when I please,
as a dragon from Shenyang
or a poster girl
            for a tattoo shop
                        named Ivy

(we will smash up we will smash up we will smash up all this beauty.)

Dominic Street, A Recipe

for Melisa Halpin

To make a beach
where there is only worn out grass
you need a lot of cider going around.

You need a cast of galloping three to nine year olds.
You need the male chest and the Chinese alphabet.
You need the sun.
You need the drone of various miniature engines.

You need two lads leaning on the railings
who can no longer speak
and have lost the fear of drowning.

Passing by in the haze
you need yourself
still wet with the belief
that beyond the light splintering on broken glass
and beneath the busted footpaths
there are seabirds,
                    ocean,
                            dolphins,
                                    sand.

Somebody's got to do Somethin...

for Kevin Higgins

Gone four O clock this was and he shitfaced out on the
balcony of the flat underneath us tryin to smash the poxy
door down with his fists BOOM BOOM SLAP BOOM
really layin into it he was and our bedroom shakin from the
floor to the ceilin our readin lamp fell over the edge of the
bedside table SMASH fuckin slivers of glass all over the
floor and course the baba woke up SCREAM and then
herself beside me started gettin very freaked out like with all
the screechin and roarin I tell you it was too much for us
too fuckin much after the day we had with the baba and
yer man below givin it socks Open that fuckin door ya jade
BOOM BOOM SMASH BOOM Open up or I'll crack
your fuckin neck for ya ya bastarin hoor BOOM BOOM
SMASH BOOM So I took a peek out through a rip in the
curtains down through the neon and the drizzle at the
lunatic below in the ripped white shirt with puke or beer
or dribble all over it t'was the husband or the partner or
whatever he was we minded our own business could o'
been her bloody life coach for all we knew BOOM
BOOM THUD BOOM BLOODY BOOM anyway
whoever he was I was sick o' listenin to the bastard a real
bully he was bein a real dictator a total fuckin Saddam the
mad moonshine eyes on him the tongue hangin out like
Jack Nicholson in The Shining the manky brown locks on
him the greasy grizzle on his chin like a friggin were-wolf
BOOM BOOM SMASH BOOM BOOM Come out of it
ya lightin cunt THUD THUD THUD THUD Open that
fuckin door ya bad bitch ya BOOM BOOM SMASH
BOOM BOOM I'm gonna rip your fuckin head off I'm
gonna shove my fuckin fist down your throat somebody had
to do somethin before he burst in and maybe throttled yer
wan and she was alright ya know always said hello and was

78

very sweet to the baba even though she'd a bit of a gra for
the gat herself like BOOM BOOM SMASH BOOM
somebody had to do somethin I didn't want it to end up
like one of those stories you read about with the rush hour
crowds streamin by lost in the music from their mp3s and
talkin into the air with their hands' free sets takin no notice
of some poor gobshite bein battered to death on the
pavement or like the way people are supposed to just draw
the curtains in London and shitholes like that when they
hear a woman screamin rape from an alleyway outside and
I thought the lock would surely give before long now
BOOM BOOM SMASH CRACK BOOM SMASH
BOOM so I dialed 999 on the moby and they put me
straight through to the Bridewell first time I ever rang the
guards about anythin and the Desk Sergeant took all the
details dead calm like and promised me they'd send a car
around soon as possible to check things out and told me to
stay inside away from the action in the meantime so we
waited and we waited and we waited and meanwhile yer
man is losin the momentum and softenin the roars windin
down to shouts the shouts windin down to pleadins the
pleadins windin down to whimpers and when I had another
goozey through the blinds he was collapsed in a heap against
the railins with the dribble and the sweat and the rain rollin
off him pathetic he was disgustin like a choc-ice meltin on
the footpah like dogshit in the midday sun then a
paddywagon screeched off the main road into the courtyard
at about seventy miles an hour brakin on a hand brake turn
SCREEEECH and four coppers hopped out of it all tooled
up like with shields and helmets and batons shufflin up the
iron steps towards yer man like special fuckin forces
Crumlin like a troop of mechanical beetles two stood on
either side of him and drew their batons and started layin
into our fuckin hero below Rodney King style CRACK
CRACK BANG CRACK whackin him on the shoulders
and up and down his back and the back of his legs with the
batons WHACK WHACK CRACK WHACK they fuckin

leathered him boy that'll quieten ya ya silly bollix who's the tough man now ha ha ha ya bleedin gobshite the coppers havin a great skit amongst themselves and yer man in fuckin agony beggin them to stop then they hauled him up onto his ass and handcuffed him and he groanin and whimperin and tried to make him stand but he would'nt or couldn't or whatever so they grabbed him by the legs and the shoulders and den the wife burst out of the door below the wan he would o murderd if he caught a holt of her half an hour ago and she bawlin at the coppers lev him alone lev him alone plee ee se plee-ee-ee-eese he's alright he's alright oh jaysus the lonesome cryin of her ye're after makin shit of him ye bastard she's all blood look at his eyes you're after blindin him this screechin really got the cops' backs up FUCK OFF BACK INTO YOUR FUCKIN HOLE BEFORE WE GIVE YOU A GOING OVER AN ALL but there was no talkin to her and maybe I should have gone out myself at that stage but sure I would have got the same but jaysus listenin to her was like a vice around my heart let him go give him back to me he's ruined plee ee ee ee eese plee ee ee ee ee se and I couldn't believe the next move could not fuckin believe it when one of the coppers swung at her with the baton and gave her such a crack CRACK right on the middle of her face CRACK the way it ricocheted around the flats the CRACK bouncin from wall to wall it must have woke a few more up and then my own baba started SCREAMIN with the terror again behind me and the mott below in the yard collapsed in a heap and the coppers pause with yer man hunched between them like a big sack of rubbish and there was a silence for a second as the coppers were all lookin backward and forward from themselves to yer wan piled there with the blood streamin out her nose until she started screamin again SCREAM bastards bastards bastards ye're after breakin my face and then the coppers were full of laughs an fuckin winks again like the Christmas fuckin party and carried on cartin Rodney the pisshead and fucked him into the back of the paddy-wagon like they were fuckin an auld armchair into a skip and then one copper turned around and he caught sight of me through the window and started starin me out of it so I just pulled the curtains over and turned out the light I felt so guilty after but I was afraid of me life and I mean I mean what could I do en'anyways I said what the bleedin hell could I do who was there to call to help that poor guy?

The Heckler

for Stephen James Smith

He was between 40 and dead and had the look of a lad who
    often wet himself,
the bed, the settee, the doorway, the ditch,
wherever he happened to land at the end of a binge.

Regarding his ponytail, I thought about roadkill,
about tyre-flattened badger, black cross-stitch down the spine
    of a fox,
about the matted stink of tar and oil and dried-out shite
    and blood,
the whoom and whoof and whine of oblivious wheels going
    over and over.

Underneath his ethnic Irish cap
the dancing wee-men of alcohol were eating his brain.
No doubt about that.
A pint of Guinness was lasting him about a minute and a half.
But he wasn't getting any merrier
no matter how many bitter black jars of it he sunk.

His days of getting happy-drunk, I guess, were over.

He leaned against the counter in the far back corner
sniggering and guffawing loud and often at his own sad snorts
    and gags,
trying to undermine the musicians and performers,
trying to clasp the crowd's attention to himself.

Not one of the 70 or 80 packed into the downstairs lounge
of the International Bar paid him more than an irritated glance —
he was so easy to ignore,
worse than useless even as a heckler.

He had the bit-o-banter with the barman though, which kept
    him yapping.
Barmen get on famously with alcoholics.
Some of them are on commission.

The heckler thought it was funny that I was from Cork.
He didn't seem to realise that the oldest and the stupidest jokes
in the world are about people from Cork.
He didn't seem to realise that making jokes about where people
    are from
or what their accents are like is to define yourself as lacking.

For me the langered Heckler is just the most boring part of
    the show.
I've dealt with a plague of them over the years.
They're really just props
giving meaning to the lives of bar stools,
shitfaced dummies interminably mouthing the script
of Old Man Alcohol, the world's hammiest ventriloquist.

Half the ones I've come across are bones.
Others go to foam with Queen Victoria in the dettol wards,
terrorised and gurgling under psychiatric sheets
in the companionless inferno of DT's.

Seized by the bleak psychedelia
of death by dipsomania
they screech at giant ants that aren't there,
at dogs with tusks and double-headed serpent tongues,
rats that thunder down the phlegm-soaked quilt like hippopotami.

Their skin and eyes burn and run.
Their young dreams vapourise.

I give hecklers all the respect they give to themselves,
which is none.

It would be convenient if there were somewhere safe and sealed off
to put these people, perhaps one of our abandoned and ghostridden
    islands,
somebody caring and skilled to see to their needs, but there isn't.
The bankers have squandered the peace and run off.
All the rest of us can go to fuck.

After the show I climbed the narrow steps out onto Wicklow St.
for some space and air. An endless queue of empty taxis
crept by, each desperate driver eyeing me up for a possible score.
I tried my best to seem penniless and like I wasn't going anywhere.

The heckler was already up there trying to sort out a deal
with a trio of drugorexic ghetto teens
who were twitching and jerking and quivering
as if connected through their trainers to an intravenous
    upper-grid
running underneath the inner-city footpaths.

It was meths or cut cocaine or speed or whatever was after
    being cooked up
that night in the flats
for gobshites;
the heckler would drop anything to keep awake and gatting.

The barman came up to assist with the negotiating.
Half-cut too, and overheated from the indoor labour, aggressive,
he threw shapes when the kids didn't like his advice.

They took the cue to rip-off the heckler for a 50 spot and scarper.
The heckler chased them up the street growling
like a half-assed bear, hoarse and limping,

but the future got away
from that outmoded bollocks
snortingly
with hands and dosh pocketed.

The heckler retraced his steps,
retreating to his public house stronghold,
to that million-chambered catacomb
which will go on robbing him till he's dead
and buried on the cheap
by our vintners' government.

Panting and bleary-eyed,
he tried to tap a yo-yo off me for a pint
but I told him to fuck off.

The Methods of the Enlightenment

My Emigration

for Ania Witkowska

I decided to emigrate to the island of St. James along with Muck, my childhood friend. We were sick of hanging around with nothing to do but occasionally go to the hospital.

We would get a job in a bamboo factory in St. James and find somewhere to live in the town of Bailey, thirty miles distant. We weren't sure if they had buses or what mode of transport was used to move the bamboo workers to and from their outside accommodations. Investigating this formed a major part of our preparatory research as we were obviously going to have to live close to a bus or train stop or whatever it would turn out to be. I hoped it was going to be a gondola system. Muck, a big Charles Bronson fan, was for helicopters, or open-backed trucks, like for melon pickers in the desert.

There were at least thirty thousand people working in the bamboo factory in St. James, which is great because when there are so many people in one place nobody can really keep track of you and you don't even have to do any work, maybe not even show up if you can get someone to clock in and out for you.

Muck would do Mondays, I would do Tuesdays, and so on; half a week each for two wages.

There is such huge demand for bamboos on the world market. I don't know why. I have never seen one.

I did some research and found that bamboos were used all over the world for things nobody is allowed to see.

Every problem is resolvable employing certain kinds of faith and determination, especially problems of the impossible.

Our problem was shoes. We didn't have any and of course you cannot emigrate without them these days. It took us weeks and weeks of shopping to find a suitable pair each. Luckily all the shoe shops in my country are conveniently placed close by to hospitals so my childhood friend could go and get his sinuses drained every day that we went shopping for shoes, otherwise he would have been so blocked up and infested he would have started to look like a septic elephant.

We got so well known in the shoe shops, and so knowledgeable on the subject of shoes, that people began asking us to help them choose shoes for them and, especially, their children. There was one particular young man who, along with his mom and poppy, was severely traumatised by an inability to find a suitable pair of shoes. They arrived into the shoe shop in a real state of cringing despair, sweating and biting their knuckles and lips. When I saw the boy I thought immediately about a pair of shoes that would suit him. A pair of blue trainers. He loved them. His mother hugged me, crying. His father had to sit down, white with relief, and I brought him a glass of brown water.

All I could think about was the factory in St. James, and the nightlife in Bailey.

On the day before we were due to go I went to the cinema while my friend went to the hospital upstairs from the cinema.

The film was a montage of my life called *Dancing With Nadrol*. It showed me at different house parties over the years in various shameful states of drunkenness and undress, falling asleep on the bosoms of women whose names I may never have known, among them a red-headed Canadian in a witch's hat, an Italian girl feeding me fat purple grapes she had grown in her hair.

It was a vortical cinema, the seats were arranged in a rotating gyrical pattern against a background of infinite black, and it was packed. I looked around and saw many people that I had helped out in the shoeshop in the previous three months since my decision to emigrate. They were all spinning around in their seats howling with laughter, torturer's laughter, at my life which was only a serious of drunken accidents and mistakes, beginning with the one that had created me.

I ran out of the cinema expecting to find my childhood friend but no. I went upstairs to the hospital, but there was such a crowd at reception there was no point. When I tried to get back out my way was blocked by a security guard with a plastic moustache. I waited until a taxi arrived for someone else and slipped out while the security guard wasn't looking. I didn't have any money for the taxi so I went to the library instead, thinking to pick up some information about St James and Bailey but as usual the staff in the library were having a party with lots of cakes and they ignored me.

My Tenure in the Whitehouse
Comes to an End

I was Sheen she threw me out finally the grump for picking at the white chocolates fore the white sauce dinner got served

Didn't think she could even see me there from the other end of the white dining hall across the white oval yoke just the two of us in white-suit white-dress at the weekly white appointment must have had her bloody eyes whitened and re-pointed. Latest in a long string of domestic disappointments I could never satisfy Nancy White in love Nancy White is a cavegirl and a thug

Like that time I was drunk with my ex-white jocks downaround mankles stumbled back heavy on the ex-white fluffy superheated toilet seat the white toilet burst causing red-brown flood and of course I couldn't plug it with my fist but the hole in the ivory floor of the bathroom wasn't I no one wouldn't was my brother Roxy smashed it quand he was dancing round stocious elephants but sure I took the blame for him as usual

That same day I spy mother white through the white arch with the vicious white lions on it pass by tiny lost in the throng of the dead of all neighbourhoods she is drunk too the way a sparrow would be drunk heading wrong way being argumentative futile pathetic flapping hot-headed flapping to convince the white life heat she isn't dead she isn't one of those dead types oh no don't the officers know who her son is get the officer in charge down here see her now let through immediately pieces of her mind let back to the land of the living special pass or else so help her bricks ton of god you'll due the ray the white life heat were having none of it didn't even answer probably get a boozy old crank like her shouting out about a presidential type son every twenty three seconds she is carried away like a twig in the currents of mud so hard to sit and watch your mother go like that but heh what can I do I got enough sparrow rescue on already close the white blinds I can order that I'm Vade Nadrol I'm the president drunk or sober

Nancy had another president in waiting ready in the wing on my way out introduced myself didn't look like me atall was a green woman white make-up much too short said Aoife was her name relatives from Donegal in Rio or Bombay in Tipperary but they stretched her legs shaved his tits and cut a face of mine from the face mountain that was that don't let them mould your face and reaperduce your expressions even leading men are replaceables. Washington's not that pleasant anyhow I wouldn't recommend I can see it ain't exactly music city now I've only got a white wine suit white hole throat white geetarmonicand my three white chords of the night-white truth so I'm on the road on the hunt easyfree ridin hobo lookin out for unwatched tracks gonna jump a pig truck gonna go rockabilly with the locks gonna head on west catchin sparks buskin off-trail all the way at the corners of Littlesquares Littlepeoples Littlevilles allsummerlong then gonna go caravan in piney Aspen ice and snow should tide me over writin songs and cookin honey mushroom hooch for the winter months waddya reckon?

The Methods of The Enlightenment

I was at high tea with a certain northern plumber, and a certain northern plumber's life coach and lover, who also does a little bit of plumbing. We were discussing our rivals in the local plumbing trade. How we could crush them. Various proposals were put forward by the life coach, who had convened the high tea, and was always eager to act as our mouthpiece.

By the time the eight-cup pot had run dry we had come round to settling on proposal number 4.

Since I am our plumbing circle's archivist, I minuted our decision in an invisible ink of our own design. On our very own invisible paper.

Recently, we have had approaches of interest in our archive from the British Plumber's Library in Harlsden centre for contemporary plumbing.

I was glad it was proposal number 4 that had won out. The other proposals were run of the mill, the usual combinations of letter-writing campaigns, anonymous e-mails and web-postings, free-for-all rumour spreading, targeted slanders, and clandestine meetings with county councillors and arts' colonels.

Proposal No 4 went like this: Invite our rivals around to our apartment to join the editorial board of a new plumbing journal of international significance, with guaranteed gold-standard funding from abroad. The beckoning of conferences galore. Give them each an alluringly fancy title as a kind of peace offering to smooth over previous attempts on their life and reputation. Say 'International Editor', or ' New Plumbing Bongo-Bongo Man' or 'Plumbetry Geronimo'. As an added bait, beg them to bring along their latest work, as much as they can fit into their satchels, for sharing and complimentary appraisal.

When they arrive, compliment them hugely on how beautiful they are in their sarongs and their various tweeds and handcrafted woollens, how distinguished looking are their sidelocks, how eyecatching is the twinkle of their chandelearings.

Separate them from their writings by telling them we are going to put the type-sheets in an anonymous pile and draw lots on the reading order, so as to be strictly democratic and equal opportunities. Put the writings safely away in the utility room.

Serve the writers canapes, and Lambrusco laced with rohypnol and valium. Tell them the vegetarian guinea pig is in the oven. Put on some hopeful ethnic music. Dance with them. Tell all of them separately that they are fabulous dancers. When, one by one, they begin to complain of exhaustion, sit them down sympathetically around a heavy fire.

As soon as they are all seated and their eyes have started to droop, beat them to death with fire extinguishers.

Afterwards, whenever we have exhausted all of our other enthusiasms and peccadillos, divide their unstained papers among ourselves, using the Methods of The Enlightenment.

The Plumbing Council

I applied to the Plumbing Council for funding for a plumber's wank.

A couple of days later I got a note back saying they were very interested, but they wanted me to come in and talk about it, and would I bring along a sample?

She was very polite, hospitable, thorough, clear, rational, efficient, consoling and evasive. She wasn't a plumber though, so she didn't know a thing about plumbing, even though she said she was a great admirer of our latest set of advanced water features. I told her she could check out my advanced water features anytime.

I hate people, and talking. They disturb me when I all I want is to be left alone at my plumbing. Anyway, what could any of us possibly have left to talk about? We're going down, and that's it. No discussion needed.

I certainly haven't got enough time left to talk about anything besides my plumbing.

We cast sighs and glances over and back at each other from across the species barrier. We were both sad because there could be no language that would suit the two of us.

After ten minutes she flopped forward onto her desk, head first. She had fallen asleep, a sign of great ambition in her line of work. Or she'd had an aneurysm. Even better. Definite promotion. Anyways, I put the sample jar down on the desk and left without a sound.

The sample wasn't mine.

The next note arrived by courier that afternoon. My request for funding had been granted by emergency session of the Plumbing Council, on strict condition that my plumber's wank be presented to the Plumbing Council assembly only, on a once-off basis, in secret session, immediately.

On the whole, the general public wasn't ready for plumbers' wanking, they felt.

That was fine by me. I don't care who's watching. Or what they do with it after I'm finished. As long as I get the pay-off.

To make it across to the Plumbing Council as soon as possible I shot the courier dead and stole his Harley Davidson. I revved it up and rode it down footpaths and cycling lanes and across the bowling lawns of old folks' homes. Some of the bowling oldies thought I was a mosquito and tried to swat me with their crutches. They threw gramophones and monocles and magic lanterns at me.

The greatest thrill was the electron-heat of the courier's bottom seeping up into my rectum from the red leather seat. The last of his life being absorbed into mine.

We were in the Plumbing Council's secret underground dungchamber. I was on stage in the dark. The spotlight was on the audience. They had arranged themselves into an organogram. The Chief Plumber was on top of the organogram in full regalia. The Chief Plumber was lean, but he was weighed down hugely by all his brass and copper medallions. The two beneath were grimacing with the effort of carrying him, the three beneath them even more so, and so on. At the bottom of the organogram there were about two hundred emerging plumbers. Some of them were under such strain their eyes had popped and their brain sponge was spilling out of their eye sockets. They had morphine needles hanging out of their necks to help them deal with the inconvenience. No way were they going to lose their places.

I explained to the audience that they, not I, would be doing the wanking. They were delighted. I said the only rule was no funny business, nothing mutual.

Everyone began rhythmically manipulating their troublesome regions as soon as I set the projector reeling. The screen showed a small silent waterfall near Cappoquin in Co Tipperary.

It worked. After a few minutes a seismic orgasm shuddered up and down the Plumbing Council organogram.

Afterwards we took time out for some audience feedback.

'Here', they chorused, 'is a plumbing with feeling in it, a plumbing that makes its audience feel something too. At last'.

C Section

for Ciarán Kelly

I can be a very bad bastard at times. I need to be to get my point across. People down my way are gone beyond reaching by any other means.

I live in a city where everyone is beautiful, dressed like they are on prime-time television, like the front covers of the magazines you find in dentists' waiting rooms, but if you wanted to talk to one of these beauty girls or boys you would have to shine a light in their eyes to check they were switched on and capable of receiving messages.

Let them at it. I have stopped trying to communicate with them anyway. It's pointless, now and always.

Sometimes I find it hard to tell the people from the mannequins they spend so much time gazing at and longing to be like.

Martyrs are the mannequins of history, plucked by vanquished and victors alike from the struggles of the past in order to make use of the perfectly malleable figures they make. They are put on show along the high streets of present ideology to the passing crowds, who stare at their own favoured martyr display through the unbreakable glass of bygone times, becoming riveted. We envy and worship our own selected martyrs for their incorruptibility, their pseudo-immortality. Yet they are always being dressed up by someone else backstage, someone still very much corruptibly alive and trying to sell us chain-garments for our minds that change their cut and shadings from season to season — to suit the dresser, not the dressed, to keep us staring in the wrong direction, to hold us enchanted.

This is how it was with Body Songs, the night before he died:

I propped myself up on the end of his prison-hospital bed, that sore-ridden rack of his famished, lingering death. Baddy must have hoped to escape from death right up until the end, unless he was just a masochist show-off wearing martyrdom as lingerie.

Escape through Victory! The prisoners XI take on the All-stars of the Wardens. With of course some outside help on shooting skills for both. What was the final score again, the tally? Anyone remember? Who won? Or was it a draw? Ah, who gives a shit in the first place?

It's like when the football game spreads from the pitch to the terraces, unmasking its true nature, the fight to the death between the warriors of rival villages. It is the fight that matters, not the spoils. We fight even when there are no spoils. The smell of the other one's fear, that's what we want, the sight of their freshly opened wounds, the music of their pleading, the taste of their blood.

We're starved for a brawl. We're hanging for a scrap.

I crossed my legs. I had a miniskirt on and I wasn't wearing any knickers and I think it would have been very unfair of me, at that point, to flaunt the fact, and possibly give poor ould Boggy Sons the horn.

Meanwhile, political corpse-fuckers stripped off and queued up in the strip-lit prison-hospital corridors, stroking their cocks to keep them rigid, like porno actors awaiting their cue at a gang-bang shoot.

I shouldn't have given a second thought to decorum, should I? I'm way too restrained for this world.

I had to shoulder all the other hunger-induced hallucinations out of the way — the harp strumming leprechauns, the various Aislings, the Virgin Mary, Joe Stalin, Robert Emmett, the poet Mangan, Christy Moore, the Banshee, Virgil, Winston Churchill etc while I was at it. They were turning up from all over for the dying, each with their different reasons for thinking to be the one Bouncy Slums would give the honour of introducing him to the eternal.

'Here', they imagined themselves declaring to some god or other, 'is a man they are naming boreens and backstreets after in places far apart as Paris and Tehran.'

We'll come back to the banshee at a later point. The Banshee, when she's in heat, when the comb is out and scraping through the knots of silver hair, is a screeching great ride.

I introduced myself. I said 'Hi Babbly, I'm Vade Nadrol.' He didn't even grunt a reply. I didn't care. He didn't have to introduce himself to me. He didn't have anything to teach me. I knew who he was. He was conserving energy at this point, calorie-counting you could call it, now that his body, through lack of nutritional input, had taken to cannibalising itself for the energy needed to keep even the basic life-pumping systems alive.

By the way I thought of the name of a great character today: 'Cannibal Blowjob'. I thought that up when I was watching Mary Poppins. Whaddya think of that?

'A spoonful of langer makes a cannibal go down, a cannibal go down, a cannibal go down....'

I taunted Bardy with two contrasting pictures of the future he would never see. He was blind by now of course, as a result of his fast unto doom, but don't let that bother you. I used mystical means to get the the images into his brain. Patented mystical means and, before you ask, not currently available on the open market.

In the first picture, the 'pink picture' in the catalogues, I showed Bonny Slings the happy, healthy, enthusiastic and open faces of the inner-city children born in a land united, socialist, intercultural and free. The women truly equal and independent, flourishing and beautiful according to their own ideas and ideals. The gentle, sober, helpful, tolerant, and humble portraits of the men, full of care and concern for themselves and others.

The other is simply called the 'black picture', although some critics, sophomorically keen to show off their obscure vocabularies, have referred to it as the 'necrotic' picture. It showed Boundary the real future, the one we are all living in. It showed him the make-up, the masquerades, the shams, the shamelessness, the lies, the failures, the cover-ups, the cheating obfuscating misdirecting leaderships on every side, the ubiquitous crap tattoos, the gypsy pogroms, the general loss of aim and direction and morale and hope, the lethargy and inertia and bitterness and divisiveness and hate, the petrifying tendrils of extinction slowly turning everything to fossil and petrol and stone, just as was now happening with Boomy.

So, I hollered, frightening all the other spooks in the room, and spooking all the frighteners, *Bony, me hearty, which one of these two visions do you think is the true one?*

An féidir liom glaoch a chur ar mo chara?

Actually, he didn't say anything. He couldn't say anything. He was dumb, and deaf, and all the rest of it, couldn't even lift a finger to point, being brain dead after sixty-five days without solids. But, don't let that bother you.

Oh, and that bin liddin' thing with the footpaths, that was my idea! I luvvvvvvvvvvv the fucking clatters, the tinny echoing!

Self Portrait in the Eye of a Horse

Is nonsense born of nonsensation?

Remainder to reflect upon the Cthulu-Kdickian hypothesis that the humaverse is an inquiry of a mechinsectoid civilization into the utility of certain physical and mental states and processes peculiar to the humaverse. Thus all humaversal events are extra-instrumentalised, and futile from any infrahumaversal perspective. Plainly said, the humaverse is a rat-in-a-cage, a hamsterwheel. It's nobodaddy's orphan, and a nothing-in-itself.

My mind is made up. So is yours.

The shiteuation so described demands nothing less than an hot air escalation on an unpresidented scale.

Right up to thermonuclear level and bebonged.

Join a unit of the electrical resistance, take up ohms on behalf of nonation.

May the cosmos have been forgotten about or abandoned or set aside whilst more important bollocks is attended to or has it been put on the back-o-me-bollocks-burner or bureaucrotically sadelined or pissed over in favour of some sycophantic ununionised arselicking alterboy or perforce it's been put into effectively infinite Waterfordian storage or it's had its funding sloshed or it's been temporarily accidentally or maliciously massplussed or for fecksake goodandall lost?

Let run on beyond its failure to result in anything worthwhile, due to a mild and anomalous interest from one or a few of The Preancestral in 'seeing what happens'?

I'd do anything for the music. Drop an E for example. Prancestors — howzat sound?

Poetry is an index of nothing outside of itself.

Medusa the maw of all mannequins is gazing deadeyes out at you from every changing room mirror, from every pair of ray-bans, from every shop-window display.

Pero, allora, forse questi che set the humaverse in motion are gone long go so even our futility is futile. We're down with Cosmoillogical Autofutility.

Neologophila is self-reflective. I could be described as a narcissistic neologophile.

Keeping the professors busy is a conservationist activity. It's a delaying tactic carried out on behalf of a friend of mine, a quark, and the last unsplit thing I know of.

One possible development is a clauseless tongue, a language of pure conjunction:

Whether for either how? But, and maybe, if once since while — although after...

I live inside a lovely divine exquisitely comfortable spacious contemporary ultra-convenient centrally located extremely well-appointed beautifully proportioned highly-recommended frequently renovated state-of-the-ark and utterly frigging worthless bubble mirror-walled throughout and obviously double-glazed and triple-locked and flood-proofed and plague-resistant and alarm-linked to o one twenty four seven three six five private snipers nestled behind every satellite dish on every ersatz terracotta roof in the neighbourhood.

Walk on I will, through all of this albumin, towards the eggshell, towards zero's edge, towards the fate of work and presidents and horses.

A resurrection in Charlesland

A resurrection in Charlesland

for Stephen Murray

> *Men are fools to invest in real estate*
>   BASIL BUNTING, "CHOMEI AT TOYAMA"

Under an avalanche of downward spikes
the flower cafe sinks

                    and could-of-beens
is all there is.

Pól Potbelly lives.

Rank-risen butchers and grocers and pigmen
have gone cuckoo in the dáil
and annexed the last of the airwaves

where they are laying a 24-7 all-channel siege
to back-up a billionaires' heave
on the commons.

It's the age of the cowboy economist

of the fire brigade turning out to be arsonists

of the world's most dickeybowed shock-jocks

of the midwives mass-trialed
with no right to reply on your laptop

of all the high-toned Pinochets
on the Radio

of a thousand and one Killiney Pinocchios

of the UCD Friedmanite
and his unchallenged pubgang of preppy echolytes

self-titled experts
in the necessary suffering of others
and how well *they* should bear it

and of a brutal commentariat

droning for national government
for slashing   whoever's timid   and convenient

                    they keep saying that

deep and swingeing cuts
must happen quick   and always,
always   *be more significant*

$$$$$$$

Here lies my anonymous address.
Charlesland.

Dormtown full of jobless insomniacs,
paupers who were affluent a year ago.

Some of many in the Stranded Archipelago

of such. Not yet a ghost estate.
Still occupied by living souls,

just.

In a nation once again
For Sale.

And our symbol?
Well, noughty Aisling's been roughed up.

The vicious alchemists of capital
put a hex on her imported make-up.

From a cocksure cocaine go-girl
she's a riddled ghetto hag.

Everyone's a patriot now,
flying their For Sale flag.

ℒℒℒℒℒℒ

All the golden nest-egg rows changed back to brick.
The hoardings' painted sunrays sprouted teeth
and claws.
In the online brochures the blue computerised skys
        were recoded
as nets that are
thickening over us.

        We're webbed up in debt
and domestic addictions.
Our white-walled kitchen loneliness
is great
        and always hungry.

Force-feeding ourselves Dan Brown, valium, parox,
Gerry Ryan and angelology,

we repeat the neo-liberal prescriptions:
staying in is the new going out
there is no such thing as society

and we swallow down the lot
with a supermarket own-brand plonk
that unmiracles to vinegar in your mouth.

             Morning after after morning after
we look back
while we're hanging
fur-tongued and possibly still langers (why not?)
        at the up-arrow years
when developers spiked us
        with a hyperstimulant called greed
with no known antidote
or comedown cure
        but death and disaster.

Estate agents casinoed our existences
spun a wheel with only one bright number on it,
Looking-After-Number-1
        kept plying the line that everyone
        was guaranteed to be a millionaire,
                for starters,

        till we were hot-cheeked with money lust
and then they swayed their magic keys in front of us
like hypnorapists goofing us
for all possible advantage.

Bankers brought the kinky costumes and equipment.
        Adpimps supplied the glitterdust and lube.
        Channel 4 filmed every oiled up inch and second of it
flatscreening it back to us
as we squatted

on the chaise-longue for years
to watch ourselves being screwed
while being screwed
on the chaise longue for years...

        and most of us knew what was happening
        and some of us truly were hoodwinked
        and nearly everybody wanted it never to stop.

Thus were we rightly sodomed here and dumped,
two million life-indentured gimps
stuck without an exit plan
          in one of time's bogged-down pauses
history's less-interesting amber phases,

dream homes become burial mounds
          in which we just about get by

                    most of the time

          without killing
ourselves or our loved ones,

square metered cells in dolmens of brick
subsiding nanometrically
in a slow motion earthquake.

          But one day we all know the cracking open will accelerate,
          the falling down around us will be far too fucking quick.
          Because isn't it obvious?

Our imitation terracotta roofs can't wait to collapse on us,
cave in becoming overnight poetic and mysterious
like all the slumped stone cottages they're jealous of,
          relics of so many oldsung irish hells
          that memorise the bitter twisted centuries before us
          and that we wist on whizzing by in cars or trains

lulled to a deep-thought serenity
by their silent exterior stillness through the window-glass
as each of them weakly yet perceptibly
          returns to us reflections
          that our inheritance is the mirror of our legacy.

          Here let me put down my stake:
          I bet you all posterity — that bingomasters' joke —

that far far future tourists visiting our formerland
as they flipper through the shoals of broken glass and
the corals on our underwater weathered brick
        will paddle lyrical about our mystical decrepitude
our enigmatic spirituality,
        our rough-hewn fortitude
in phrasings no-one now alive could hope to understand

and they will be delighted not to have the chance
to know what you and I
actually felt
because sensation is what truly dies.

Brick and even word a while survive
        but pain
has no remembrance.

Pain is now.

Pain is all the stretched out moments
        you must just go on
living through

while your muddle years
are being sucked

                into finance's bodiless hole

and your swinging retirement is hauled off
in a secret convoy to a noplace
for disacknowledgement,

        an offshore no-address
somewhere west of Easter Island
        with all the rest of the lost lottoed lives
and forfeited futures of Charlesland.

        A no recoverable haven.

Think! Memory!
The globe of time spins round upon
a carousel of catastrophe.
Our joust is coming round, again.
Who will ride and who be ridden?

The million damn-blasted cottiers
paragraphed in your textbooks
are not just your ancestry.

They are your childrens' ravaged shadows
catching up with
and becoming
your children.

Our grandchildren's days
        will be worse
        than our nightmares could dream of.

€ € € € €

Christmas zooms
because Christmas is a zooming season.

Family close in.

Pixelated friends of ghettosuburbs gone are sudden
flesh and musk and yep yap yup again
just like Mike TV.

The 365 Xpress
hurtling irreversibly
towards A and E terminus —
standing-room-only —

dissolves at the stop
while it's dumping me off

as full and as empty
as when I got on it

$$$$$$$

and how those Kens and Barbies in the Crescent penthouse
can still afford to throw a 12 day cocaine orgy

at which everyone is fucking elephants

when all the Chalkdust Charlie's been metabolised
and flushed away to stupefy the riverfish

eventually

them gang solicitors will
I sweat to God
levitate butt-first
and be whooshed off
in an UFO

like a black yacht
or a Stealth or the Holy Spirit

to New Ould Ireland in the Outback
or the Huron or Dubai

with powdered millions in their rectums

to fuck-kill some other slaves there
get themselves
replacement gums and septums

€€€€€€

to latin treks   and altitudes   and jungle wars
decapitated roadside borderland Does

twelve   hundred   unguarded
south-western coves
all mourning glory and nose-annah be

interbreeding panics multiply
epidemics spume through pipes and Gaps
from Blessington reservoir
and the backstreets of Bray

with their royal republican monikers
Albert Walk, Wolfe Tone Square,
a seaward alleyway called Connolly

where Junkies shit, shoot-up
and die grammatically
in looping pre-recorded sentences of death

as if death's browned off with death
nothing left to say upon
the ultimate subject of itself

geriarchs as flaccid-fat as seals
dropping off in black and white
beneath remaindered paperbacks
on fin-de-siècle seaside holidays

skull and crossbones on a kite
the sighing ageless sea
floating kids and
donkeymen

brass-band-skeletons

lightning
glints like shells on the horizon of quartz

through the whole submarine the oberlieutenant's bronchial cough

or death being born-again reformed
in famished strung-out multiples
along the motorway

in a skinning hood's
reversing testicles

a collallapsing doll's
backsliding ovaries

her shitfaced unitoothed barflea uncle
a quartermaster in the Chuckies
gave away the mysteries
of the uphill avenger a.k.a mercury tilt
to a founding looder of the INLA

and it's thanks to Tony, Bertie and the mid-fall USA
that the peacetime lá and dividend has come

to these two leg tarantulas
with strictly business petrol bombs

$$$$$$$

The wise guys in the headshops
are running low on scientific miracles

having just provoked
a snowed-in soiree
in the Grove

— late night revellers
zanier on unproved chemicals
than a thousand Timothy O Lears —

to let fly an emergency flare

that swallowed the moon and puked up a blanket
of cold electricity

indifferently smothering the stars

££££££

in number 47
two tokes on the postman's *Divinorum*
opens a wraith-hole to the Salviazone
where wind-chimes are buzzin like saws in the Amazon

and something gnomish but sparkling
and scheming far harder
is speech bubbling sinister hieroglyphics
to strangely gyring russian dolls
as they circulate among the eel-crowd

with their stringalong faces and garments of worms

£££££

gaping shadow cries

$$$$$

losts
of ghost estates
sempiternally must mourn
all futures past

achieving of
the neverborn

€€€€€

And could things be worse?
Of course, of course
said the horny black horse.
In the all alone field it was eating.

At least we're still breeding.
Guinness books of unprophylated spunk
spouting out through our divining pumps
the ovulations raging

$$$$$$

On a moonlit mountainside in No 58 upstairs
by lakes of crinkled foil and absolüt
under clouds of lavalamps with lightning tentacles

MBA Tina still whirls in her upper class dreams
her vapourising expectations

a quaking rut in an oak chateau
with an upright and parlying wolf
whose prick can sing librettos
in simultaneous RussianArabFrench

while downstairs on the rocker-cum-guest bed by Lidl
Georgie hums a medley of Lady Ga-Ga, Christy Hennessy
    and Handel
in a cock-eyed trance
an ecstasy of unimpeded masturbation

as he scores the cursor back and forth
across the genital hors-d'oeuvres
and sub-sub-sub-menus on *slutload.com*

pronging through the teeny gang bangs
he's a clicking connoisseur of
and when alone with other men
an opinionated critic of as well

$$$$$$

Twenty sets of curtains and a wooden fence out west along

the small dark wood that forms the gap
between private and public estates

the bonfire eeaawws and amadáns
shotgunning Bavaria's run-off
flagon-bonging *Incense* and *Sniff*
and the *Genuine Gold*

would lacerate the Luciferan throat, be Jaysus

shove that in your pope and mitre it

says he

while Urbi's eating Orbi out

of his tree

££££££

The over sixty-fives are being strongly advised
by the shock weatherwoman
not to venture out this heart-chilling year
except for mass and visitations

the weather's unholy, prehistoric, perfect for mammoths
and statues

mares are going bronze on the hillsides of Wicklow
sheep lying down in the folds of geology

stranded cattle crystallise in drifts
foxes brittle in the fossilising winds

rock outcrops are raisins on the iced flanks of Camenabologue
and Tonelagee

and bones are snapping all around me

it is a trying time for insurance executives
there are far too few ambulances

€ € € € € €

The host, I chuckle to myself, *is eating corpses*

xxxxxx

Every family electrocutes their back-yard rowan sapling

pookabuds beaming with
vanilla-leaf, assumption blue, peachy tea,

rosé glimmerers

pretty for a night or two but sure then
sure then it's like hanging out your rubbish

though I stop

        every time
to drink

        the silver shimmer
at the tree of glass.

$$$$$$$

Wheelie bins of every crawling creep and colour
celebrate together
ecumenically

lid-lips glistening and sweetly-sour with poultry fat
and week old cream of brandy

streams and screams of their fluorescent laughter

their subsonic belching at the culinary joy of so much refuse
at how they've done the competition

built the stock
to break the neck
of any unionised binman

£££££££

The childkillers in Superquinn play Slade repeat
and Wham and Huey Lewis and the News on infinite

until Wham! — American Psycho appears
slashing backwards and forwards through the aislefuls of shite
we will all have to pay for
again and again

waving his brute insignia
the heraldry of present times

the almighty axe
of his restructuring

€ € € € € €

90 is the crack and speed at which Tadëuz
smacks the Crescent wall.
Redundant carpenter from Lodz.

£££££££

Christmas grows old quicker than fabled men get turned
    to stone

dies slurping its own waste
as if shit were the elixir

gross and indolent and pucker-lipped

thick with bling

burping its last fart

$$$$$$$$$

my head my head my head my head

my head my head my head my head

my head my head my head my head

my head my head my head my head

my head is a fucking goldfish bowl

its five second memories

circle gleaming
flat-eyed and innocent

virused senseless
by the poisoned-information overload

they suffocate
go down
into the all-encroaching blackout zone

€ € € € €

and it is the last and final
take-away chicken supper

and all night I am destined to suffer
the martial jealousy of fireworks

sure they are small and trash against the night
as childishly as toddlers pot and can the kitchen floor
but they are all the fathers of firestorms

and the alarms triumph over every human sound

saving David Bowie's little geniekin
sobbing on the pavement

his-her running glamourpus
like someone maliciously photoshopped
by a fucked-over ex

a clown with the face
of a used-up palette

a goo mask
found in a pile on Francis Bacon's studio floor

not sure if he's a teenage rape or rapist

when here comes a security guard burglar with 10000 volts
in the nightstick of his cock

and the year shuts down like a manhole on a sack

sudden unassuageable

boom

and

clang

echoing

while

the horizon pointlessly resorbs
the last unfertilising star
into its scheduled slot
in the globe spanning nought

and Jan First struts out of the unhinging year
in chainmail and mace
with clipboard and smartphone and second hand lash

cruel Sgt of the dawnless, the light-bled

to threaten and to goad

me over the top of every morning in the world
towards trenches and managerial objectives in China

and TOMORROW STINKS TOMORROW STINKS
TOMORROW STINKS TOMORROW STINKS

tomorrow stinks like a tricoloured Cod

tomorrow spills the deep sea's blood
upon the playgrounds and the pebbledash

tomorrow salts the Sugarloaf
tomorrow cancels poetry and physics

and the only true promise I can make to my tomorrowgod
is to be as
resolute and
as heartless and as
boiling with love and the apocalypse
as anybody's sun and lord

About the author

Dave Lordan was born in Derby, England, in 1975, and grew up in Clonakilty in West Cork. In 2004 he was awarded an Arts Council bursary and in 2005 he won the Patrick Kavanagh Award for Poetry. His collections are *The Boy in The Ring* (Cliffs of Moher, Salmon Poetry, 2007), which won the Strong Award for best first collection by an Irish writer and was shortlisted for the Irish Times poetry prize; and *Invitation to a Sacrifice* (Salmon Poetry, 2010). Eigse Riada theatre company produced his first play, *Jo Bangles*, at the Mill Theatre, Dundrum in 2010. He has lived in Holland, Greece and Italy, and now resides in Greystones, Co Wicklow. He can be contacted at dlordan@hotmail.com.